What THE DOCTOR Smokes

NH
NEW HOLLAND

Contents

Introduction

So what *does* the doctor smoke? Pretty much anything, if you believe the adverts in this book! Yes, when these doctors aren't busy telling us to drink whisky and eat sweets, they're falling over themselves to endorse their favourite cigarettes. Sometimes elbowing sports stars out of the way to do so ...

It's not just the way the medical and sporting professions were used to sell unsuitable products that seems strange to modern sensibilities – can you imagine a modern dieting aid advert headed 'Fat Folk'? Or even an advert for bread that features a huge, growling, scary wolf?

And if you think the means of selling is odd – look at the products themselves! They range from a belt that electrocutes its wearer to provide 'vigour' to a 'chin reducer and beautifier' contraption that looks more like a torture device.

Funny and ridiculous as they undoubtedly are, deliberate humour doesn't play a big part in these adverts, maybe because it's only in retrospect that we can see that Dri-Poo for the hair might not be the most savoury of names, or that a horse exercise machine (guaranteed satisfaction) might find its real market in sexually-frustrated Victorian housewives.

But perhaps the real reason the adverts in this book make us laugh out loud is because they come from eras with completely different ideas and values from ours – where pesticide-covered oranges were a good thing and sunlamps were genuinely used to ward off the flu in children.

And that's the warning these adverts should give us. We may think we're more sophisticated now, but under all the gloss of modern marketing, has much really changed? Next time you're convinced you need the latest must-have product, look back at this book and beware!

Drink for health

Alcohol has always been used for medicinal purposes, but you don't get many adverts nowadays that sell it as a curative first and foremost, before the 'fun and relaxation' element, or the 'get out of your tree and forget the mess you've made of your miserable life' one. Still, it's a lot easier to justify buying whisky by the caseload if it's your medicine cabinet you're re-stocking, rather than the drinks one. Not that the people in these adverts are a great recommendation for the health-giving properties of booze – they're mostly either decrepit or boss-eyed …

1900
M. D. Daly and Sons Advert

Pouring it through a funnel doesn't make it medicine,
but you can't blame the old boy for trying.

**1910s
Hall's Wine Advert**

This advert might
have a fair enough
claim if it wasn't for
her cross eyes.

**1920s
Whiteway's Advert**

An apple a day
keeps the doctor
away. And
apparently the
same is true if it's
an alcoholic apple.
How convenient!

**1930s
Dewar's Advert**

Wonder if there's a
similar cure for
bird flu? Fingers
crossed!

**1900s
Newball and
Mason Advert**

Mason's essence is
non-alcoholic,
which is just as well
if you serve it at
kids' parties by the
gallon.

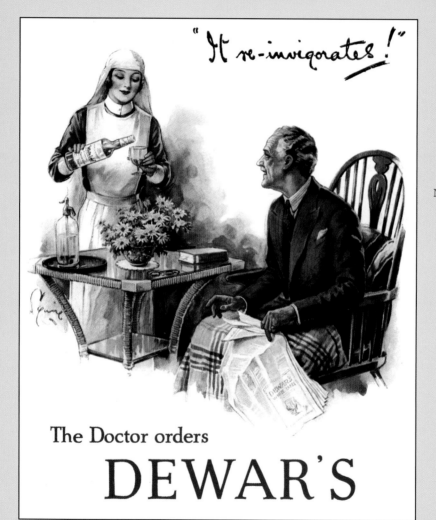

"*It re-invigorates!*"

The Doctor orders

DEWAR'S

**1933
Dewar's Advert**

Now that's the kind
of doctor's advice
I like!

**1950s
Seagers Advert**

After drinking a mixture of egg and wine, swinging her around like that might not be the best idea.

**1958
Rheingold Advert**

Madelyn loves a
beer before she
jumps in her car.
Just hope that dog
moves out of the
way quick enough.

**1890s
Antidipso Advert**

And if you're still
not convinced that
drink is good for
your health, why
not try Antidipso?
Just slip it in his tea
and watch him
jump back on that
wagon!

DRUNKENNESS CURED.

It is now within the reach of Every
Woman to Save the Drunkard—A Free
Trial Package of a Marvellous
Home Remedy Posted to All
Who Write for it.

**Can be Given in Tea, Coffee, or
Food, thus absolutely and
secretly Curing the Patient in
a Short Time without
his knowledge.**

There is a cure for drunkenness which has shed a radiance
into thousands of hitherto desolate firesides. It does its work
so silently and surely that while the devoted wife, sister, or
daughter looks on, the drunkard is reclaimed even against his
will and without his knowledge or co-operation. The Company
who have this grand remedy will send a sample free to all who
will write for it. Enough of this remedy is posted in this way
to show how it is used in tea, coffee, or food, and that it will
cure the dreaded habit quietly and permanently.

A lady residing in Manchester used the remedy as described
above, and her experience, told in her own words, will quite
likely interest all women deeply. Mrs.——— says: "Yes, I used
Antidipso without my husband's knowledge, and completely
cured him. He was a hard drinker, a good man when sober,
but for years I lived in fear and dread, shame and despair,
poverty and disgrace. How shall I tell other women about
it? Is it not a wonderful thing that a woman can take matters
in her own hands and stamp out this dreadful curse to the
home? I am glad you are going to publish my experience,
for then I know it will reach hundreds of other poor souls,
and they will cure their husbands just as I cured mine. I
am so grateful for the marvellous changes that have come
into my life that I just feel I would do anything to let every
wife and mother know what a blessing Antidipso is. I
honestly believe it will cure any drunkard, no matter how far
down he may have fallen.—Faithfully yours, Mrs.———."
(Full address sent to bona-fide applicants.)

Hundreds of others are reported, even the worst cases where
the habit seems to have blotted out the last remaining spark
of self-respect. Tears and prayers are of no use. Pleading,
pledges, loss of social or business position are unavailing to
stem the tide of absolute depravity.

This famous remedy has reunited thousands of scattered
families; it has saved thousands of men to social and business
prominence and public respect; has guided many a young
man into the right road to fortune; has saved the father, the
brother, the son, and in many cases the wife and daughter, too.
Such a godsend to the home should be known to everyone.
Upon application to the **Ward Chemical Co., 10,
Century House, Regent Street, London, W.,**
they will post a free package of the remedy to you, securely
sealed in a plain wrapper, also full directions how to use
it, books, testimonials from hundreds who have been cured,
and everything needed to aid you in saving those near and
dear to you from a life of degradation and ultimate poverty
and disgrace. Send for a free trial to-day. It will brighten
the rest of your life.

You too can look like a model

Inner beauty is for ugly people. It's a superficial world we live in so if you want to make the most of what nature gave you, then take a look at the informative adverts that follow. Yes, certain gorgeousness awaits you once you've strapped one of these not-at-all-cumbersome contraptions around your head, smothered your face with one of these categorically non-poisonous lotions or swallowed a few of these oh-so-tasty-sounding tablets. Want to lose weight? Beef up your muscles? Grow some hair? Not a problem; it's all easily within your reach if you just send a prompt cheque to the address given …

1890s
Medical Battery Co. Advert

Troubled with the 'female ailment' of hysteria?
It's easy to stand up straight when you've got a
cattle prod down your back.

CURVES OF YOUTH

will be yours if you will

"Pull the Cords"

Gives the
Flesh the
Resiliency
and
Freshness
of
Youth

PROF.
MACK'S

Chin Reducer

and

Beautifier

Prevents
Double
Chins

Effaces
Double
Chins

Reduces
Enlarged
Glands

The only mechanism producing a concentrated, continuous massage of the chin and neck, dispelling flabbiness of the neck and throat, restoring a rounded contour to thin, scrawny necks and faces, bringing a natural, healthy color to the cheeks, effacing lines and wrinkles. Price only $10. What better investment could be made? Sent postpaid immediately.

Free Booklet

—giving valuable information on how to treat double chin and enhance facial beauty will be sent on request. Write at once to

Prof. Eugene Mack

507 Fifth Ave.   Suite 1004   New York

**1890s
Curves of Youth
Advert**

Much as this looks like a torture device, it is actually the secret to a youthful look. A youthful horse, that is.

MADAME ROWLEY'S TOILET MASK.

TOILET MASK
OR
FACE GLOVE.

The following are the claims made for Madame Rowley's Toilet Mask, and the grounds on which it is recommended to ladies for Beautifying, Bleaching, and Preserving the Complexion:

TOILET MASK
OR
FACE GLOVE.

First—The Mask is Soft and Flexible in form, and can be Easily Applied and Worn without Discomfort or Inconvenience.

Second—It is durable, and does not dissolve or come asunder, but holds its original mask shape.

Third—It has been Analyzed by Eminent Scientists and Chemical Experts, and pronounced Perfectly Pure and Harmless.

Fourth—With ordinary care the Mask will last for years, and its VALUABLE PROPERTIES Never Become Impaired.

Fifth—The Mask is protected by letters patent, and is the only Genuine article of the kind.

Sixth—It is Recommended by Eminent Physicians and Scientific Men as a SUBSTITUTE FOR INJURIOUS COSMETICS.

Seventh—The Mask is a Natural Beautifier, for Bleaching and Preserving the Skin and Removing Complexional Imperfections.

Eighth—Its use cannot be detected by the closest scrutiny, and it may be worn with perfect privacy, if desired.

Ninth—The Mask is sold at a moderate price, and is to be PURCHASED BUT ONCE.

Tenth—Hundreds of dollars uselessly expended for cosmetics, lotions, and like preparations, may be saved its possessor.

Eleventh—Ladies in every section of the country are using the Mask with gratifying results.

Twelfth—It is safe, simple, cleanly, and effective for beautifying purposes, and never injures the most delicate skin.

Thirteenth—While it is intended that the Mask should be Worn During Sleep, it may be applied WITH EQUALLY GOOD RESULTS at any time to suit the convenience of the wearer.

The Toilet Mask (or Face Glove) in position to the face.
TO BE WORN THREE TIMES IN THE WEEK

Fourteenth—The Mask has received the testimony of well-known society and professional ladies, who proclaim it to be the greatest discovery for beautifying purposes ever vouchsafed to womankind.

COMPLEXION BLEMISHES

May be hidden imperfectly by cosmetics and powders, but can only be removed permanently by the Toilet Mask. By its use every kind of spots, impurities, roughness, etc., vanish from the skin, leaving it soft, clear, brilliant, and beautiful. It is harmless, costs little, and saves its user money. It prevents and removes wrinkles, and is both a complexion preserver and beautifier. Famous Society Ladies, actresses, belles, etc., use it.

VALUABLE ILLUSTRATED TREATISE, WITH PROOFS AND PARTICULARS.

—MAILED FREE BY—

TOILET MASK
OR
FACE GLOVE.

Send for Descriptive Treatise.

THE TOILET MASK COMPANY,
1164 BROADWAY,
NEW YORK.

Send for Descriptive Treatise.

TOILET MASK
OR
FACE GLOVE.

Mention this paper when you Write.
[1887]

**1890s
Madame Rowley's
Toilet Mask
Advert**

Hannibal Lecter has nothing on this woman.
Yet apparently the Toilet Mask 'cannot be detected by the closest scrutiny'. *Unless* you happen to notice the huge straps covering her head and the weird skin, of course.

A PERFECT LOOKING NOSE

CAN EASILY BE YOURS.

Trados Model No. 25— British Patent—corrects all ill-shaped noses quickly, painlessly, permanently and comfortably at home (diseased cases excepted). It is the only adjustable, safe and guaranteed patent device that will actually give you a perfect looking nose. Over 89,000 satisfied users (ladies, gentlemen and children). For years recommended by physicians. 17 years' experience in manufacturing Nose Shapers is at your service. Write for free booklet which tells you how to obtain a perfect looking nose

M. TRILETY, *Specialist,* **Rex House, D.542, 45, Hatton Garden, London, E.C.1.**

1900s
M. Trilety Advert

If only all those people who've had nose jobs
had known about this amazing device – so easy!
And so attractive!

1900s
Jonteel Advert

It's always a worry, that you'll put on your night cream and wake up with a full-grown beard. But fortunately for this lady, Jonteel 'will not grow hair on the face'. Phew!

**1900s
Aspinall's Advert**

It's slightly
unnerving when
a product has to
tell you it won't
poison you.

FAT FOLK

Should take **FELL'S REDUCING TABLETS.**

Registered by Government.

A Remarkable Remedy

That Reduces Weight 28 lb. a month.

Every person who is suffering from too much fat can easily be reduced in weight by this new and remarkable remedy that quickly removes all superfluous fat in either sex at the rate of **7 LB. A WEEK.**

It is guaranteed to **Reduce Weight a Pound a Day** without the slightest inconvenience. Do not be afraid of evil consequences. It is a vegetable treatment, is perfectly safe, and gives such a degree of comfort as to astonish those who have panted and perspired under the weight of excessive fat. It improves the breathing, gives the heart freedom, takes off the big stomach, enables the lungs to expand naturally, and you feel a hundred times better the first day you try this wonderful

HOME TREATMENT.

"Getting Fleshier Every Day."

Lost 40 lb.

Lady —— writes: "Since taking your tablets I am reduced in weight 40 lb.

Thousands of Testimonials sent on request.

FREE

Just to prove how effective, pleasant, and safe this remedy is to reduce weight, we are sending free trials. If you want one send us your name and address and two stamps to pay for postage. It costs you nothing to try it. Each box is sent in a plain sealed package, with no advertisement on it to indicate what it contains. Correspondence strictly confidential. Address: Fell Formula Association, 20 Century House, Regent Street, London, W.

1903
Fell's Reducing Tablets Advert

'Takes off the big stomach'. Perhaps Ryvita might
like to borrow that for their adverts?

YES!
DRI-POO
Certainly Improves My Hair!
Have you tried it yet?

The New Way to Fluff and Clean the Hair

DRI-POO is a delightful preparation and so good for the hair. Excess oil, dandruff, "dirt" and all foreign matter instantly respond to a Dri-Poo treatment. Use it as often as you wish. It is harmless. Just loosen the hair with your fingers, fill with Dri-Poo and brush out. That's all. And the result is hair sweetly clean, fluffy and in the best dressing condition.

We will send a small size can of Dri-Poo to your home postpaid for 25 cents or 50 cents for the large size, if you will mention the name of your merchant.

Our booklet, "The Crown of Beauty," which we will send free on request for the name of your merchant, tells how to prevent discolored, faded, brittle and falling hair, and also gives valuable hints about dressing the hair.

J. J. WITTWER   Seattle. Wash.

**1920s
Dri-Poo Advert**

Oh dear, this is an unfortunate name. Or maybe it's not and they really are suggesting rubbing desiccated crap in your hair.

**1920s
Vreeland Advert**

This man is frightening. Do not send him your address. No hair is worth it.

1920s Alois Merke Advert

Alois is going to be a busy (not to mention bushy) man – growing hair for *all* his customers …

**1930s
Perihel Advert**

Does your
child need
'vitaminising'?
Have you tried
cooking her under
a sunlamp for a
few hours?

For 1940 —
Be Fit & Slim

Every woman wants to look better, to feel better in the year ahead. Slenderness is the way to health, beauty and fitness. A couple of Bile Beans taken nightly enables you to 'slim while you sleep'— surely and safely.

These fine vegetable pills do more than disperse unwanted fat— they purify and enrich the blood, tone up the entire system and make you feel better in health in every way.

So start with Bile Beans to-night and make sure of looking and feeling your best in 1940.

By Taking
BILE BEANS

SOLD EVERYWHERE BRAND PILLS

**1940s
Bile Beans Advert**

Mmm … bile beans. How very tempting. And if they repeat on you afterwards, they'll taste exactly the same.

**1940s
Ironized Yeast
Tablets Advert**

Thanks for that, Gil. Looks a little bit like you've just drawn two made-up pictures – one skinny and one beefy – but I'm sure that's not the case.

**1947
Speritt Advert**

'If I close my eyes tight enough, mum might stop giving me skin cancer.'

**1970s
Cabot Sloane
Advert**

Transformation indeed! She's not only changed from 'fat and lonely' to 'slim and desirable', she's also gained a third dimension and no longer resembles Chewbacca.

Smoking is good for you

Smoking gets a bad rap these days, what with the lung cancer, the hacking cough and the bad breath … Not so in the late 19th and early 20th centuries. Back then, cigarettes were everyone's favourite friends. Doctors, dentists, sportsmen, singers and film stars: they were queuing up to lend their names to the cigarette companies' ad campaigns. Each brand was keen to stress that their cigarettes were the ones to relieve your hoarse voice, prevent you from binge eating and stop your teeth resembling Shane MacGowan's. When adverts featured glamorous women, athletic men and kindly old doctors, who wouldn't be convinced?

1890s
Cigares de Joy Advert

You might think a child with asthma needs an inhaler, but apparently not – Joy's cigarettes were great for kids!

Pass a <u>B.D.V.</u> CIGARETTE
between your finger and thumb and
notice how perfectly the Tobacco is
packed in it.

The long strands of tobacco are perfectly compressed to admit
of perfect combustion ; there are no loose bits of tobacco to
irritate the palate or the throat ; and there is that full measure
of leaf which gives full value and full weight.

B.D.V. Cigarettes
can be Smoked All Day.

They are perfectly pure and dustless, and their flavour
and aroma can be enjoyed without palling on the palate.

**Buy a tin to-day and test their superb
quality.**

*Enquiries from the Colonies and abroad should be
addressed to Export Department, 60-62, Commercial
Street, London, E.*

2/2

Sold in Tins of 100.

If you are unable to obtain them at your Tobacconist's,
send 2/2 for sample tin of 100, post free, to the
manufacturers—

GODFREY PHILLIPS & SONS,
112, Commercial Street, London, E.

**1910s
BDV Advert**

BDV cigarettes 'can
be smoked all day'
– although surely
that interferes with
other harmless
activities? What
about constant
gin drinking?

**1910s
Craven A Advert**

Ah, those were the days, when doctors recommended not just 5-a-day of your fruit and veg but also 20-a-day of his favourite fags.

What the Doctor Smokes

The doctor's choice in tobacco is CRAVEN Mixture, and he is supported in that choice by the verdict of the greatest medical journal in the world—

"The Lancet"

which published on August 24th, 1912, an analytical report showing that of all well-known tobaccos CRAVEN is unmistakably the purest and best, the smoke of other well-known tobaccos yielding **7 to 10 times, and some tobaccos 16 times, as much nicotine** as that found in CRAVEN. Therefore the doctor smokes and should recommend CRAVEN Mixture as the **best** for **health.**

The purity and sweetness of CRAVEN are due to the special process possessed only by Carreras, Ltd., and by which all impurities and crude nicotine are removed.

CRAVEN MIXTURE is made under the same formula as when immortalised by J. M. Barrie as "Arcadia" in my "Lady Nicotine," and it contains nothing but pure tobacco.

On sale all over the world. In cartridges or loose in tins 2oz.1/3
CARRERAS, LTD. (Est. 1788), Arcadia Works, City Rd., London, E.C. & Montreal, Canada. West-end Depot : 7, Wardour St. Leicester Sq. London, W.

PUNCH, OR THE LONDON CHARIVARI.—December 4, 1929.   xv

IT'S BETTER TO BE FIT THAN FAT

Don't eat between meals

EATING between meals causes fat, and fat destroys your waistline — your fitness—your energy. Here's a simple pleasant way to overcome the craving for between-meal bites — it's the Kensitas way. Every time you have the temptation to eat between meals — *don't do it* — **smoke a Kensitas instead.** There's a mellow satisfaction in the appetising aroma of a Kensitas. You'll be delighted to see how quickly the Kensitas way eliminates the desire to eat between meals. Try it — you'll like it!

MANUFACTURED BY THE
KENSITAS
PRIVATE
PROCESS

10 *for* 6ᵈ – 20 *for* 1/-

"As good as really good cigarettes can be"

Your **Kensitas** *Cigarettes Sir*
REAL VIRGINIA

**1929
Kensitas Advert**

Not a bit of advice you'll find in most modern diet books.

**1930s
Lucky Strike
Advert**

Sex sells. And, er,
so do doctors by
the sound of it.

Her Singing Coach Advised A Light Smoke

CAROLE LOMBARD* PREFERS LUCKIES
BECAUSE THEY'RE EASIER ON HER THROAT

"When I had to sing in a recent picture," says Carole Lombard, "I considered giving up smoking. But my voice teacher said I needn't if I'd select a light smoke—Luckies.

"I soon found that even when singing and acting 12 hours a day, I can smoke as many Luckies as I like . . . without the slightest throat irritation."

The reason Luckies are easy on Miss Lombard's throat is because the process "It's Toasted" takes out certain throat irritants found in all tobacco—even the finest.

And Luckies do use the finest tobacco. Sworn records show that among independent tobacco experts—auctioneers, buyers, warehousemen, etc.—Lucky Strike has twice as many exclusive smokers as have all other cigarettes combined.

In the honest judgment of those who spend their lives buying, selling and handling tobacco...with men who know tobacco best . . . it's Luckies—2 to 1.

*Star of the new Paramount production "True Confession"

A Light Smoke

EASY ON YOUR THROAT—"IT'S TOASTED"

WITH TOBACCO EXPERTS...
WITH MEN WHO KNOW TOBACCO BEST
It's Luckies 2 to 1

1930s Lucky Strike Advert

What the ad doesn't mention is that Carole is singing baritone in a Welsh Miners' Choir.

1932
Murad advert

It's important for a company to identify its target
market – Murad obviously thought its was
'careless drivers who don't like confrontation'.
Seems a little narrow, but Murad knows best …

**1930s
Kensitas Advert**

Don't you just hate
the man who dares
to cough when
surrounded by
smokers? How
rude!

**1930s
Lucky Strike
Advert**

Who'd have
thought that
snacking between
meals was the
downfall of this
aspiring hurdler? If
only he'd had a
40-a-day habit.

**1930s
Cooltipt Advert**

Who knew wool
was so effective?
That must be why
you don't see
sheep with
smokers' coughs.

1940s Camels Advert

Perhaps the most worrying thing about this ad is what the doctor with the microscope is looking at – and whether that particular patient's test results revealed they were in fact made of fag ash...

NOTED THROAT SPECIALISTS REPORT on *30-Day Test of Camel smokers...*

Not one single case of throat irritation *due to smoking* CAMELS!

Yes, these were the findings of noted throat specialists after a total of 2,470 weekly examinations of the throats of hundreds of men and women who smoked Camels— and only Camels—for 30 consecutive days.

FRED ASTAIRE reports: "I MADE MY OWN 30-DAY MILDNESS TEST. IT'S CAMELS FOR ME FROM NOW ON!"

Start your own 30-Day Camel MILDNESS Test Today!

CAMEL
TURKISH & DOMESTIC BLEND CIGARETTES
CHOICE QUALITY

The inimitable Fred Astaire has been King of the Dance for as long as most theatre-goers can remember. Fred calls time for a Camel as he works out a new ballroom routine at the famed Fred Astaire Dance Studios.

R. J. Reynolds Tobacco Co. Winston-Salem, N. C.

"*Camels agree with my throat!*"

JEAN PUGSLEY, secretary, who made the 30-Day Test under observation of a throat specialist, says, "Camels agreed with my throat from the start!"

"LONG BEFORE I got my doctor's report, I knew Camels agreed with my throat. Milder cigarette I ever smoked!" Robert Murphy, production man.

LEONA STEVENSON, saleswoman: "I smoked many different brands before I discovered the one cigarette that really agrees with my throat—Camel!"

"I MADE THE TEST and my doctor's report was no surprise to me. Camels agreed with my throat from the very first puff!" Joe Govor, salesman.

HOUSEWIFE Mrs. Edna Wright: "I made the doctor's test. It was fun! Camel mildness certainly agrees with my throat. Wonderful flavor, too!"

"I STARTED smoking Camels because they taste good. I've kept on smoking them because Camels agree with my throat!" R. M. Elliot, merchandiser.

1940s Camel Advert

If Fred's 30-a-day mildness test convinced him, that's good enough for his glamorous assistant!

**1940s
Viceroy Advert**

Never? Perhaps
they mean stain
them white ...

"I'm going to grow a hundred years old!"

...and possibly she may—for the amazing strides of medical science have added years to life expectancy

● It's a fact—a warm and wonderful fact—that this five-year-old child, or your own child, has a life expectancy almost a whole decade longer than was her mother's, and a good 18 to 20 years longer than that of her grandmother. Not only the expectation of a longer life, but of a life by far healthier. Thank medical science for that. Thank your doctor and thousands like him... toiling ceaselessly, often with little or no public recognition... that you and yours may enjoy a longer, better life.

According to a recent Nationwide survey:

More Doctors smoke Camels
than any other cigarette!

NOT ONE but three outstanding independent research organizations conducted this survey. And they asked not just a few thousand, but 113,597, doctors from coast to coast to name the cigarette they themselves preferred to smoke.

The answers came in by the thousands... from general physicians, diagnosticians, surgeons—yes, and nose and throat specialists too. The most-named brand was Camel.

If you are not now smoking Camels, try them. Compare them critically. See how the full, rich flavor of Camel's costlier tobaccos suits your taste. See how the cool mildness of a Camel suits your throat. Let your "T-Zone" tell you (see right).

THE "T-ZONE" TEST WILL TELL YOU

The "T-Zone"—T for taste and T for throat—is your own proving ground for any cigarette. Only your taste and throat can decide which cigarette tastes best to you... how it affects your throat. On the basis of the experience of many, many millions of smokers, we believe Camels will suit your "T-Zone" to a "T".

CAMELS *Costlier Tobaccos*

1940s Camel Advert

Notice how the top section of this advert has nothing to do with the bottom? But maybe she will live forever... as long as she stays away from those cigarettes her doctor's so keen on.

**1940
New White Owl
Advert**

So that's where Tim
Henman's been
going wrong – not
as many cigars in
his training plan.

STRAMONIUM CIGARETTES HELPFUL IN ASTHMA

as reported in the British Medical Journal, August 15, 1959

Noted allergist reinvestigates an old treatment for bronchial asthma

For about 150 years Europeans have inhaled smoke from burning stramonium leaves to relieve asthmatic attacks.

Now a noted allergist reports in the British Medical Journal that results of controlled studies leave no doubt that inhaling stramonium (atropine*) smoke has a beneficial effect on the function of the lungs in bronchial obstruction.

The results indicate that smoking stramonium cigarettes has a definite place in the treatment of asthma, increasing the vital capacity and giving a feeling of relief, without unpleasant side effects. In many cases during the controlled study the patients voluntarily commented on their increased ease of breathing.

Stramonium cigarettes have been manufactured by R. Schiffmann Co. for more than 80 years and have been *available without prescription in every drug store* throughout the U. S. and Canada under the name of ASTHMADOR. These cigarettes contain no tobacco and are not habit forming.

ASTHMADOR is also sold in pipe mixture or as aromatic incense powder. Sufferers from bronchial asthma will almost invariably find relief, as indicated in this report.

Atropine is the alkaloid of stramonium.

1960s Asthmador Advert

Stramonium is now known to be toxic – surely being poisoned would be classed as an 'unpleasant side effect'?

1975
Tipalet Advert

An unusual pulling
technique, this one.
Or perhaps that's
chloroform he's
blowing at her
and she'll be out
in seconds?

Blow in her face and she'll follow you anywhere.

Hit her with tangy Tipalet Cherry. Or rich, grape-y Tipalet
Burgundy. Or luscious Tipalet Blueberry. It's Wild!
Tipalet. It's new. Different. Delicious in taste and in aroma.
A puff in her direction and she'll follow you, anywhere.
Oh yes... you get smoking satisfaction without inhaling smoke.

Smokers of America,
do yourself a flavor.
Make your next
cigarette a
Tipalet.

New from Muriel.   About 5 for 25¢.

You are what you eat: a donut

Healthy eating is nothing new. It's just that back in the first half of the 20th century, 'healthy eating' meant stuffing your face with sweets and fizzy drinks – hooray! Sounds like much more fun than boring old fruit and vegetables …

But while a lot of these brands are healthy-enough foods that are still going strong today, their advertising has grown up a lot in the last 70 or so years – you won't see many snarling wolves or sad and raggedy-looking urchins in modern adverts, more's the pity.

**1890s
Grove's Advert**

In the 1890s, being as fat as a pig was obviously something to be envied. Why isn't that the case any more, alas?

1890s
Hovis Advert

It's an interesting approach from Hovis to use a
huge growling wolf to sell their bread. Wonder
why it's not more common?

1911
Quaker Oats Advert

The dirty, scraggy-looking one on the left or the goblin-ears child on the right?

**1917
Allenburys Foods
Advert**

Same boy aged 32
years: undergoing
therapy after having
embarrassing baby
snaps shown
to world.

**1920s
Dr Bundensen
Advert**

Well? Do you? Best have another KitKat Chunky, just to be on the safe side.

**1931
Skipper's Advert**

Did his mother warn her about the 'repeating'? Perhaps that's why she's so keen on filling him with sardines.

**1930s
Libby's Advert**

Gee whiz, how fun is breakfast in this house? I'm guessing it's not the 'sauerkraut' flavour that he's drinking, or he wouldn't look nearly so happy.

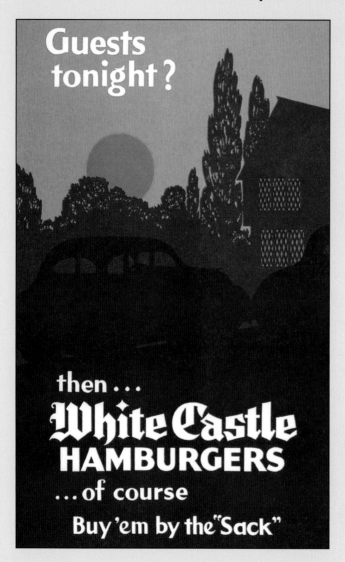

**1940s
White Castle
Advert**

The entertainer of the 1940s had it right – why slave over a hot stove when you can buy your dinner in a sack?

**1942
Skinless Advert**

This chap loves his sausage sandwich! Plus eating sausages to defeat Hitler sounds a lot easier than the other option ...

FOOD POWER will help Win the War

Sausage is FOOD POWER!

FOOD POWER BUILDS MAN POWER to do a war winning job. Eat for Food Power because the "U. S. Wants Us Strong." Follow Uncle Sam's Nutrition Program. Every day eat meat, poultry or fish, fruit, vegetables, bread, cereal, milk, cheese, butter or other spreads. These foods contain Food Power . . . and sausage and SKINLESS frankfurters are concentrated meat foods that are delicious and good for you. They contain vitamins, complete proteins, carbohydrates and minerals. 100% edible . . . no waste . . . easy to fix . . . help meal planning.

THERE ARE MANY KINDS OF SAUSAGE, SKINLESS frankfurters and wieners. Each with its own appetizing flavor and goodness in sandwiches, cold and hot meals. Leading packers now protect the food value and flavor of sausage in clear, sparkling "VISKING" casings . . . a cellulose covering you'll recognize instantly. However, the "VISKING" casings are removed from SKINLESS frankfurters and wieners. The surface you see is formed by the wiener itself in the smoking process.

YOUR DEALER KNOWS SAUSAGE, SKINLESS frankfurters and wieners. His stock includes many kinds and brands to fit your needs. Buy wisely so that your meals will always have "Food Power."

SERVE THIS NUTRITIONAL MEAL
MADE WITH

Skinless
TRADE MARK
FRANKFURTERS OR WIENERS

. . . creamed carrot casserole and deviled eggs. Include other foods recommended in the U. S. Nutrition Program.
Having no skins, SKINLESS frankfurters and wieners cook quickly, don't split open to lose their food value and flavory juices.

THE VISKING CORPORATION • 6733 WEST 65TH STREET, CHICAGO, ILLINOIS

"VISKING" is the registered trade mark of The Visking Corporation   Copyright 1942, The Visking Corporation

JOHN BULL March 12 1955

YOU won't find this family going without a meal if they can help it. Certainly not the one at the end of the day! So, as you can see, they are a thoroughly healthy, contented bunch. With one of those sensible mothers who knows the more her family enjoy a meal the more good it does them.

Home to that good meal they need!

4 out of 6 women know how to make a good meal wonderful

Serve Batchelors Peas! Serve them with beef, or lamb, or pork. Serve them with fish. Have them in casseroles. In salads. Never be without Batchelors Peas. And why Batchelors, you ask? Simply because they're *always* nicer. And so say 4 out of 6 women!*

A nation-wide survey showed that of all women who named their favourite brand of peas, 4 out of 6 named Batchelors.

Batchelors PEAS
make a good meal WONDERFUL

BPP 44/40
44

**1950s
Batchelors Advert**

Yes, that's right, mum's fed up of looking after you lot so it's nothing but peas from now on.

60

**1950s
National
Confectioners
Association Advert**

Personally, I use
up my 'Can Do'
sitting in front of
EastEnders, but it's
good to know I'm
replacing lost
energy and not just
stuffing my face
with Haribo.

1950s Cynamid Advert

This child doesn't look convinced by the pesticide-covered juice. Although maybe she's just mesmerised by her mother's magnificent eyebrows.

How chemistry is saving your orange juice!

Last summer an invasion of the Mediterranean Fruit Fly threatened to destroy Florida's huge citrus crop. Prompt action in spraying thousands of acres with malathion, the remarkably versatile insecticide developed by American Cyanamid Company, is achieving control. As a result, millions of dollars worth of citrus fruits and juices are being saved for America's breakfast table! Here is a dramatic example of how Cyanamid's chemical developments are helping the farmer protect and increase our nation's crops—to serve and conserve in making the fullest possible use of the country's agricultural resources. AMERICAN CYANAMID COMPANY, 30 Rockefeller Plaza, New York 20, N.Y.

**1900s
Beecham's Advert**

All this eating can play havoc with a girl's digestion. But never fear, Beecham's laxatives will sort things out, leaving you with that attractive 'I've been to the loo twice already today' look.

Miracle cures

Feeling a bit down in the dumps? Lacking in vital energy? Then look no further than your nearest plug socket. Yes, back when domestic electricity was new and exciting, consumers were clamouring to buy the latest belt, brush or appliance that would provide them with the revitalising wake-up call of an electric shock. Strange but true. Still, it makes a change from yeast.

But perhaps the greatest example of gullibility seen in these miracle cures is whoever seriously believed that the horse exercise machine was an innocent home work-out …

1880s
Dr Scott's Advert

No need to backcomb your hair with this little beauty; use the electric brush and watch your hair stand on end.

1890s
A. M. Richardson Advert

Wonderful discovery! Wear this magnet to get
rid of 'impure blood'. Warning: side effects
include clothes falling off.

**1890s
Page Woodcock's
Advert**

'Oh, this is so
exciting, having my
portrait painted …
What did you say
I'll be advertising
again?'

**1890s
Harness Advert**

No more sticking
leeches on your
eyes. In that case,
even an eye
battery sounds
like a good idea.

**1890s
Brain Salt Advert**

The Pro-Plus for
the 19th-century
student – Brain Salt
promises a certain
cure for 'excessive
study'. Another
is *Trisha*.

HORSE EXERCISE AT HOME.

By Royal Letters Patent

Vigor's Horse-Action Saddle

TROT, CANTER, & GALLOP.

VIGOR LONDON

PERSONALLY ORDERED BY

H. R. H. THE PRINCESS OF WALES.

Her Excellency the Countess of Aberdeen *writes:* "That the Saddle has given her complete satisfaction."

The ADVANTAGES of this UNIQUE SUBSTITUTE for Horse-Riding are:

It promotes health in the same degree that Horse-Riding does.

It invigorates the system by bringing all the **VITAL ORGANS** into **INSPIRITING ACTION.**

It acts directly upon the **CIRCULATION**, and prevents **STAGNATION OF THE LIVER.**

It is a complete cure for **OBESITY, HYSTERIA,** and **GOUT.**

LANCET :—" Both the expense and difficulty of riding on a live horse are avoided. The invention is very ingenious."

FIELD :—" We have had an opportunity of trying one of the VIGOR'S Horse-Action Saddles, and found it very like that of riding on a horse ; the same muscles are brought into play as when riding."

WORLD :—" It is good for the figure, good for the complexion, and especially good for the health."

PARTICULARS, TESTIMONIALS, and PRESS OPINIONS POST FREE.

Vigor & Co. 21, Baker St. London.

1890s Vigor & Co. Advert

Ahem. It seems the Countess of Aberdeen is 'completely satisfied' by her horse-action saddle. Lucky her.

1900s
Dr McLaughlin
Co. Advert

This belt apparently provides 'courage'. Or maybe others are just scared by the constant buzz emanating from your middle.

ELECTRICITY VICTORIOUS

Amazing Results with Electrical Treatment in the Home.

INFINITE JOY OF HEALTH

Although universally accepted as being the most powerful curative agent in existence, many sufferers have yet to learn of the extraordinary powers of the new treatment by which curative, life-giving, and revitalising Electricity can now be applied in the home by means of simple appliances, which even a child can manipulate.

The wonderful "AJAX" Dry-Cell Body Batteries infuse new life and energy into your weakened body; they drive out pains and aches, and restore your bodily functions to a perfectly healthy condition.

A SCIENTIFIC FACT

The reason why is very simple; the motive power of the human machinery is Electricity, and when through excessive strain, overwork, or chronic complaints this natural strength has been overdrawn upon, the functions get out of gear, and suffering is the result; you become but a shadow of your former self, weak and debilitated. But give back to your body what it has lost, and so surely as an electric bell starts ringing immediately you press the button, if the CURRENT IS THERE, so will you recover health, strength and well-being if you will renew your store of Electricity to its proper level. If you overdraw your account at the bank the matter is remedied by supplying fresh funds. That is exactly the point: refill your overdrawn system with its life power and all will be well again.

All the greatest scientists endorse our contention that Electricity is the very life of the human body, and therefore you must investigate this unfailing means of regaining the infinite joy of vigorous, robust health.

80 PAGES BRIMFUL OF KNOWLEDGE

That is our booklet, entitled "Electricity the Road to Health." Write for it at once, TO-DAY, and you will learn how a host of complaints are successfully overcome; Weakness in all its forms is vanquished; Rheumatic, Neuralgic, and every other pain dispelled for ever; Indigestion, Constipation, Liver, Kidney, and Bladder troubles cured, never to return; Brain-fag, and all nervous complaints completely eliminated. This small book will cost you nothing, but may be worth a fortune to you. Write for it now, whilst you have it in mind, or call if possible at the Institute, when in a personal consultation you will be told exactly what can be done for you, free of charge, and get a free test and examination of the appliances. AJAX LD.

Do not "Put off"; call or write at once for full particulars.

THE BRITISH ELECTRIC INSTITUTE (Dept. 163), 25 Holborn Viaduct, LONDON, E.C.1

1910s
Ajax Advert

This Ajax battery cures constipation – not a huge surprise. You try not going when you're being electrocuted.

Why catch their Influenza?

Y OU need not! Just carry Formamint with you and suck these delicious tablets whenever you are in danger of being infected by other people.

"Suck at least four or five a day"—so says Dr. Hopkirk in his standard work "Influenza"—for "in Formamint we possess the best means of preventing the infective processes which, if neglected, may lead to serious complications."

Seeing that such complications often lead to Pneumonia, Bronchitis, and other dangerous diseases, it is surely worth while to protect yourself by this safe, certain, and inexpensive means. Protect the children, too, for their delicate little organisms are very exposed to germ-attack, especially during school-epidemics. Be careful, however, not to confuse Formamint with so-called formalin tablets, but see that it bears the name of the sole manufacturers: Genatosan, Limited (British Purchasers of Sanatogen Co.), 12, Chenies Street, London, W.C.1. (Chairman: The Viscountess Rhondda.)

"Attack the germs before they attack you!"

Though genuine Formamint is scarce your chemist can still obtain it for you at the pre-war price—2/2 per bottle. Order it to-day.

Formamint
THE GERM KILLING THROAT TABLET

1918
Formamint Advert

The flu epidemic of 1918 killed millions, but clearly not those sucking Formamint!

NEURASTHENIA CURED BY ELECTRICITY.

WONDERFUL CURES OF NERVE WEAKNESS, DEBILITY, AND NERVOUS DYSPEPSIA.

TO-DAY, the conditions of life are causing a serious increase in Neurasthenia and other nervous and Functional disorders. The symptoms of Neurasthenia are many and varied. They are mainly mental or nervous, and often the victim is quite unaware of the fact that he or she is travelling rapidly towards Nervous Exhaustion and Nervous Prostration.

HAVE YOU ANY OF THESE SYMPTOMS?

Are you Nervous, Timid, or Indecisive?

Do you lack Self-Confidence?

Do you dread Open or Closed Spaces?

Are you wanting in Will Power?

Are you "Fidgety," Restless, or Sleepless?

Do you Blush or Turn Pale readily?

Do you shrink from Strange Company?

Are you subject to Sudden Impulses?

Do you crave for Stimulants or Drugs?

If so, you can safely assume that you are suffering from Neurasthenia. The Neurasthenic also often suffer from **Indigestion, Liver Troubles, Constipation, Palpitation, Loss of Appetite, Excess of Appetite,** and a host of other disorders due to faulty functioning of various organs. Electricity is the only force that naturally supplies this deficiency of Nerve Force, and restores tone to the whole nervous system.

The greatest neurologists, including Erb, Beard, Loeb, and hundreds of the foremost medical thinkers, now agree that electrical treatment, skilfully and scientifically directed, will revitalise depleted nerve centres (as in

ARE YOU NERVOUS LIKE THIS?

If so, Curative Electricity will put you right. The Pulvermacher Appliances are the only inventions for the administration of curative electricity, endorsed by over fifty leading Doctors and by the official Academy of Medicine in Paris.

neurasthenia, debility, and nervous dyspepsia), restore sound digestion, invigorate the circulation, and increase the daily and necessary elimination of the waste products that, if uneliminated, are the greatest source of all diseases.

To-day you can be

CURED IN YOUR OWN HOME BY ELECTRICITY

by simply wearing the Pulvermacher appliances, which are light, easy, and comfortable to wear. They give no shock, but all the time they are being worn they supply the nerve centres with a continuous flow of electricity, naturally stimulate the circulation of the blood and increase nerve nutrition.

This is the natural and physiological treatment of Neurasthenia, which drug treatments can never cure. The Pulvermacher Treatment has cured the most obstinate cases of Neurasthenia and Nervous Disorders when all other methods have failed. If you are suffering from any form of Nerve Trouble, or if you have any of the symptoms as here described, write to-day for a book that may well prove of incalculable health value to you, yet it costs you nothing. It is entitled "Guide to Health and Strength," and will be sent post free.

Those who can call personally are cordially invited to do so, when a consultation on their health trouble may be secured absolutely free of charge and without obligation between the hours of 10.0 and 5.30 daily.

FREE COUPON

By posting this **FREE FORM TO-DAY** you will receive the "**Guide to Health and Strength**." You place yourself under no obligation by applying for this Book and particulars of the Pulvermacher Appliances.

Name...

Address...

....

Post to the Superintendent, Pulvermacher Electrological Institute, Ltd., 81, Vulcan House, 56, Ludgate Hill, London, E.C. 4.   *The Sphere, January 25, 1919*

1920
Pulvermacher Electrological Institute Advert

Don't waste your time being scared of the car, old guy – you're stood next to Lightbulb Man!

**1920s
Dr West's Advert**

Jim was doing well to keep his relaxed and easy manner when faced with the terror of sogginess.

The PASSING SHOW, July 15, 1933   (Supplement)

Don't You Feel Well Mummy?

How Can You Tell Them You Feel

EXHAUSTED NERVY, HEADACHY, WEAK, DYSPEPTIC, LISTLESS, Thoroughly RUN-DOWN & OUT OF SORTS?

*T*HEY know "something" is wrong—but they don't realise how ill you feel! They don't know how you WEAR YOURSELF OUT looking after them, how the daily tasks seem to sap every ounce of your vitality, how their noise and chatter makes your head ache and throb—tears your nerves to shreds! But we know how the cares of motherhood wear down the strongest system. We know how you feel—that is why we tell you to take "Yeast-Vite" Brand Tonic Tablets.

TAKE 2 OR 3 YEAST-VITE TABLETS AND FEEL FIT AND FRESH IN A FEW MINUTES

—Why continue to be agonised by Terrible Headaches, Niggling Nerve Pains, Black Depression, and Heavy-Limbed Lassitude?

—Why go on denying yourself the Gift of Sound Digestion, Steady Nerves and Unflagging Energy when you can experience the benefit of this marvellous Lightning PICK-ME-UP?

Yeast-Vite has conquered. It has come as a marvel of relief to Tired, Exhausted mothers. It has restored Brightness to the Eye and Youthful Bloom to Pale, Wan Cheeks. It has given Energy to men where before was the hopeless, listless anguish of Nagging Headaches and Worn-out Nerves.

"Yeast-Vite" regulates the action of the Digestive Tract. It relieves and banishes Dyspepsia. And in cases of Anæmia, Sleeplessness, Stomach Troubles, and Constipation it works absolute wonders.

For "Yeast-Vite" supplies to your body just those essential elements of well-being which a Run-down and Pain-racked system needs. In this accurate Scientific Combination of Pure Medicinal Yeast (Saccharomycetis Cerevisiae), Valuable Vitamins and other Tonic Ingredients is a concentrated source of New Life, New Health and Vigorous Vitality for YOU.

YOUR QUICK-HEALTH TIME-TABLE

FROM	TO	TIME
NERVE PAINS -	Glorious Relief	In 5/15 MINS.
HEADACHES -	Deliverance	In 5/15 MINS.
LASSITUDE -	Vim and Vigour	In 10/20 MINS.
DEPRESSION -	Buoyant Energy	In 10/20 MINS.
"NERVES" -	Steadiness	In 10/°0 MINS.
INDIGESTION -	Keen Appetite	In 15/30 MINS.
EXHAUSTION -	Animation	In 15/30 MINS.
SLEEPLESSNESS	Calm Repose	In 30/60 MINS.
RHEUMATISM -	Pain Relief	In 24 HOURS
CONSTIPATION -	Regularity	In 36 HOURS
IMPURE BLOOD	Purification	In 36 HOURS

NO CURE — NO PAY

Simply obtain a 1/3 bottle of "YEAST-VITE" Brand Quick-Tonic Tablets from any Chemist. Try the treatment at our risk, and if you are not THOROUGHLY CONVINCED of the WONDERFUL POWER

PERFECT SAFETY, and TONIC PROPERTIES of "YEAST-VITE," return the empty carton to Irving's Yeast-Vite Ltd., Watford, and your money will be refunded in full.

Yeast-Vite BRAND

Quick-Tonic Tablets. All Chemists, 3d., 6d., 1/3, 3/- & 5/-

T.C.R.

1930s YeastVite Advert

Oh no, thoroughly run-down? How rotten! What you need is YeastVite, a certain cure for annoying children.

1930s Fleischmann Advert

'It's difficult to do your work and keep pleasant'. How true, Jones, how true.

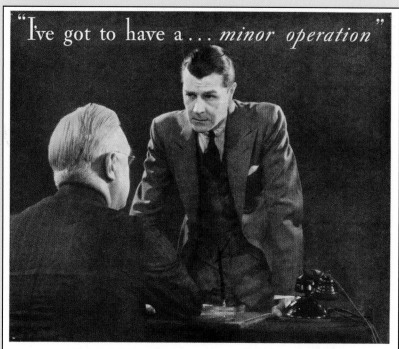

"I've got to have a . . . *minor operation*"

More serious than most men realize . . .
the troubles caused by harsh toilet tissue

In nearly every business organization a surprisingly large percentage of the employees are suffering from rectal trouble.

This fact is well known to companies that require physical examinations of their personnel. Yet even these same concerns are frequently negligent in providing equipment that will safeguard the health of their employees.

Harsh toilet tissue, for instance.

Any physician will tell you that mucous membrane can be seriously inflamed by the use of harsh or chemically impure toilet tissue.

Some specialists estimate that 65 per cent of all men and women at middle age suffer from troubles caused or aggravated by inferior toilet tissue.

Protection from rectal illness is just as important in the home as in business. Fortunately, women are more careful in matters of this kind than men. Already millions of homes are equipped with ScotTissue or Waldorf—the tissues that doctors and hospitals recommend.

Extremely soft, cloth-like and absorbent, these safety tissues cannot harm the most sensitive skin. They are chemically pure, contain no harsh irritants.

Be safe . . . at home, at work. Insist on Scot-Tissue or Waldorf. Scott Paper Company, Chester, Pa. In Canada, Scott Paper Company, Ltd., Toronto, Ontario.

SCOTTISSUE, *an extremely soft, pure white, absorbent roll containing 1,000 sheets*
2 for 25¢
Price for U. S. only

Soft as old Linen
ScotTissue
The absorbent soft white Toilet Tissue
Scott Paper Company
Chester, Pa., U.S.A.

Waldorf
A Scott Tissue

WALDORF, *soft and absorbent, yet inexpensive*
Now 6¢ a roll
Price for U. S. only

Stores displaying this sign HEALTH PRODUCTS are featuring Health Products during June and July
Featured at this store!
It will pay you to buy in quantities

1930s
Waldorf Advert

What on earth is he *doing* with his loo roll? And are they seriously suggesting you ask your employers to change their brand of toilet tissue?

**1930s
J. W. Simpson
Advert**

... and for our next
product, magic
beans!

NOW she is *immune* from 'Flu, Colds or any epidemic for 12 months because she is wearing the Simpson Iodine Locket

Whilst worn, the Iodine is constantly breathed into the system through the skin pores for 12 months (the life of the Locket).

Men wear the Locket in the vest pocket.

More than 2,500,000 wearers have in this way been kept free from 'Flu, Colds, Catarrh and Rheumatism.

This is Mr. J. W. Simpson, Chemist, the Iodine Specialist, Inventor of the "IODOLOK" Iodine Locket.

The Locket is sold by all Chemists, 1/9 each, 3 for 4/6. But see the name and the word "IODOLOK" embossed in gold on the Locket, as there are some cheap imitations about.

J. W. SIMPSON (CHEMIST) LTD., ALDWYCH HOUSE, LONDON, W.C.2

27

A woman's work is always fun

Before the evil cloud of feminism cast its shadow over so many happy homes, encouraging women to leave their housework and wear dungarees instead, little ladies the world over were busy having fun washing up and vacuuming. They liked nothing more than to receive a household appliance for Christmas and serve up a delicious meal of canned soup to their hungry husbands. Occasionally, they even troubled their pretty little heads with the world of work, where they had much fun typing up clever men's business (goodness knows what it was all about, but when their typewriters were so nice and colourful, who cared?)

A WARNING

to girls who work in offices

Nervous strain increases perspiration—
don't run the risk of "undie odor"

Please do not expect employers or even office mates to warn you of this hard-to-forgive offense.

Girls who work in offices are so apt to run the risk of unpleasant "undie odor." Naturally so, because everybody perspires more under nervous tension. And underthings are constantly absorbing perspiration acids and odors. Others notice this before you do.

Don't take chances that may spoil your business success. There is one sure way to *know* you're fresh and sweet. Lux removes "undie odor" *completely*, yet so gently that colors and fabrics are never harmed.

It's delightfully easy to Lux your lingerie and stockings after *every* wearing. Then you avoid all embarrassment, all risk of offending. This dainty habit takes only 4 minutes, or less!

Try Lux FREE! Try this wonderful care for your lingerie, at our expense. Just send us your name and address, and by return mail you will receive a full-sized package of Lux free. Write today to Lever Brothers Company, Dept. BX-5, Cambridge, Massachusetts.

Risking her job?

Clever, efficient, her loyalty and hard work are surely appreciated. Yet this offense is too serious—no one could overlook it. If only some one could warn her that she is risking her job!

LUX

Pretty Hands
Lux in the DISHPAN leaves hands soft, snow-white. Costs only 1c a day!

LUX for underthings—
keeps them like new in spite of frequent washing

**1930s
Kellogg's Advert**

Yes, and the more
comments like that
a husband makes,
the more likely he
is to go to work in
dirty socks.

1930s
Lux Advert

Got that? Men can't fall in love with a woman
who offends!

Clever
Wife

she knows that
men like soups
···and hearty soups!

Ever notice the look of sunny contentment
that comes into a man's face after he has eaten
a plate of good hot soup? You might almost
call soup the chief aid of anxious wives because
it's so certain to be what the man wants to eat
first, when he comes home tired and hungry.
Something that tastes mighty good, and goes
right to the spot—*quick*.

You have just the answer in Campbell's
Soups—off the shelf—on the range—in the
plate—all in a twinkling. You can tell at the
first spoonful he likes it—and how! It has the
rich, sparkling flavor that chases his frowns and
makes him appreciate you as a "cook." Especially
when you select one of those extra-substantial
Campbell's Soups which are "naturals" for the
male appetite. The suggestions below are sure
to help you when you visit your grocer.

Soups men like ··· *a few* **Campbell's** *favorites*

Oh, Wednesdays and Fridays
Are great nights for me,
With Campbell's broadcasting
Such laughter and glee!

**CAMPBELL'S
ON THE AIR!**

Fridays
Dick Powell's "Hollywood Hotel"
—all-star revue—9-10 P.M. (E.S.T.)
Columbia Network—coast-to-coast.

Wednesdays
George Burns & Gracie Allen
—new program—8:30 P.M. E.S.T.
—7:30 C.S.T.—9:30 M.T.—8:30 P.S.T.
Columbia Network—coast-to-coast.

NOODLE with chicken —
A feast in "honey" goodness which
no man, woman or child can resist.
It just teems with chicken richness
(broth and meat)—and those fine egg
noodles which delight the hunger.
Here is an "old-timer" glorified by
Campbell's into one of the most
popular soups of today. Just taste it!

OX TAIL—
A hit with men—and everyone with
a vigorous appetite. It's a richly meaty
soup with its own world-famous
flavor—yet seldom attempted in the
home kitchen. Campbell's bring it to
you at its best—selected ox tail joints,
invigorating meat broth, nourishing
vegetables — deliciously combined.

PEPPER POT—
The real Philadelphia kind, so famous
in old Colonial days and ever after.
It gives you a splendid chance to vary
your soups with a welcome and delightful novelty. Beef broth, macaroni
dumplings, meat, potatoes, onion,
ground black peppercorns, marjoram,
thyme, sweet pimientos—what a soup!

VEGETABLE-BEEF—
The true old-fashioned vegetable
soup which contains tempting pieces
of meat. You can depend upon it as
a sure attraction to the man in the
house. It's so hearty and satisfying
— so abundantly supplied with meat
and vegetables and barley—a meal
in itself. And for the children's lunch
or supper, nothing could be better!

LOOK FOR THE RED-AND-WHITE LABEL

**1930s
Campbell Advert**

Clever?! For a start
she's serving soup
on a plate, which is
never a good idea.

**1936
Listerine Advert**

Poor old stinky Edna. Can you imagine a more horrifying prospect for a woman than being unmarried in her late 20s?

1950s
Horlicks Advert

Come-hither Horlicks? Well it's certainly a lot
easier than stockings and suspenders…

**1940s
Climax Advert**

Now she has her Climax, washday's her favourite day of the week. Funny that.

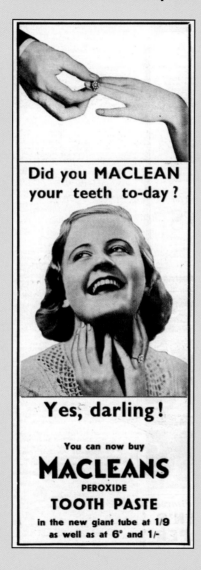

**1952
Macleans Advert**

Good, because if
not the wedding's
off quicker than
you can say 'Is that
a lump of spinach
between your
grotty teeth?'

**1940s
Tern Advert**

And what makes a
perfect man?
Someone who
pretends to love
getting another
boring shirt for his
birthday?

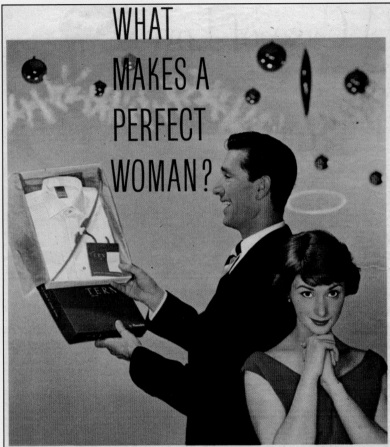

WHAT MAKES A PERFECT WOMAN?

Do you freeze with him at football matches? Brave the 'jalopy'—and *blow* your nylons? Suffer sock-darning with a smile? Good! You get 7 out of 10. Now go for full marks. (Easy!) Just give him a TERN. Definitely the gift he'll *adore* you for, every time he wears it. (You'll love him in it, too). *Wonderful* shirt. Never needs ironing. Always looks smart. Bliss for bachelors! Ready to give—with your love— for only **39/6.** In white, cream, blue, grey or green never-iron poplin. Buy him a TERN *today.*

CHRISTMAS TIME—TERN TIME

TERN
Trade Mark *by Consulate*
NEVER-IRON POPLIN
M. Bertish & Co., Ltd. London, N.15.

To Gladden Hearts and *Lighten* Labor

DOWMETAL···THE WORLD'S LIGHTEST STRUCTURAL ALLOY

Almost a score of years ago Dow undertook to produce American made magnesium alloys—the metal that is a full third lighter than aluminum.

Then, and through the years, Dow looked forward to the day when the startling lightness of this metal would make a myriad of tasks easier for mankind.

First to take advantage of Dowmetal was the aviation industry where its unique lightness combined with strength is of untold value.

Gradually it found acceptance in industry—adding speed to machine parts, cutting power costs, aiding transportation and speeding manual operations.

Finally, a year ago, Dowmetal entered the household appliance field through its adoption by The Hoover

Company for the famous Hoover One Fifty Cleaning Ensemble. So audible has been customer enthusiasm for the amazing lightness of that product that Hoover designers determined to incorporate this feature in the just-announced lower priced Hoover Model 25.

Obviously, Dow has long since overcome those problems of production which stood in its developmental period as economic barriers to wider use. Moreover, recent advances in fabrication, notably high speed die-casting, enable users of Dowmetal to adapt it to their production methods on a close-cost basis.

Thus, the ambition for Dowmetal is now realized. It is serving industry in an ever broadening capacity and finding its way into the homes of people—to gladden their hearts and lighten their labors.

THE DOW CHEMICAL COMPANY, MIDLAND, MICHIGAN

Branch Sales Offices: 30 Rockefeller Plaza, New York City • Second and Madison Streets, St. Louis • 135 South La Salle Street, Chicago

DOW

CHEMICALS INDISPENSABLE TO INDUSTRY

1950s Dow Advert

Seconds after the blindfold came off, the vacuum cleaner was wrapped around Mr Smith's head.

**1950s
Sky-line Advert**

Lucky girl indeed!
Although any
woman this
attached to her
knives is probably
in anger
management
classes.

Lucky Girl!

she's got *Sky-line*
'CHEF' CUTLERY
– it's hollow-ground

'Sky-line' new Chef hollow-ground cutlery
is getting a warm welcome from housewives
for it's really good looking, utterly practical
in the kitchen . . . and is so reasonably priced.
Such a variety of knives meet every cutting
need, with Sheffield stainless steel blades—
hollow-ground for lasting sharpness and smart
rosewood handles to give you a comfortable
grip. Attractively boxed, these modern aids
in the home make wonderful gifts too. You
can also choose individual knives from the
self-service 'Sky-line' display at your dealers.

These are the popular 'Chef' sets by 'Sky-line'

4005 5-piece set as illustrated above
(Paring, Utility, French Cook's,
Carving and Bread Knives) ... Price 30/-
4032 2-piece carving set (Carving Knife
and Fork) ... Price 15/6
4026 3-piece carving set (Carving Knife,
Fork and Steel) ... Price 25/-
4043 3-piece boxed set (Carver, Bread and
French Cook's Knives) ... Price 21/6
4033 Carded set (Cook's, Utility and Paring
Knives) ... Price 10/11

Also obtainable as single pieces from 2/11 at your favourite
store or ironmonger.

Hightime you had Skyline   *they start sharp–stay sharp*

By the makers of (**Prestige**) housewares

If your husband ever finds out

you're not "store-testing" for fresher coffee...

...*if he discovers you're still taking chances on getting flat, stale coffee ...woe be unto you! For today there's a sure and certain way to test for freshness before you buy*

Here's how easy it is to be sure of fresher coffee

Look for the "Dome Top" Can of Chase & Sanborn. That firm, rounded top shows it's packed *under pressure*, fresh from the oven.

Just do this:

Press your thumbs against the dome top *before* you buy. If it's firm, it's fresh. If the top clicks, pressure's gone—take another. It's the one way to get the freshest coffee ever packed.

No other can lets you test!

You can't test an ordinary flat top can. Some are "leakers" that have let air in to steal freshness. But all flat top cans look alike. You can't tell which are good and which are stale.

Here's the payoff!

Sure as you pour a cup, they'll want more! For Chase & Sanborn is a glorious blend of more expensive coffees ... brought to you *fresher*. No wonder Chase & Sanborn pays a flavor dividend you won't find in any other coffee!

REGULAR GRIND
PRESSURE PACKED
Chase & Sanborn COFFEE

"PRESSURE PACKED"

Chase & Sanborn

103

**1950s
Chase & Sanborn
Advert**

And if he catches you using tea bags instead of loose, he'll lock you in the cupboard for a week.

1950
IBM Advert

If this is really her idea of a perfect day, then she is on some serious medication.

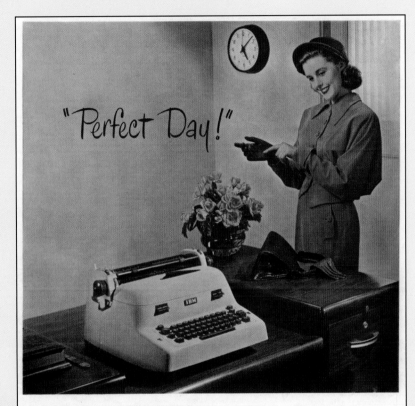

"Perfect Day!"

Typing all day is easy and effortless when you have an IBM Electric. All you do is "touch" the keys—the typewriter does the work. At five o'clock you'll still feel fresh and free from fatigue.

You'll like all the energy-saving features of the IBM Electric, its simple operation, its perfect impressions, its modern styling. You'll like having the world's finest typewriter for your own.

IBM, Dept. B 3
590 Madison Avenue, New York 22, N. Y.

☐ I'd like to see a demonstration of the IBM Electric Typewriter.

☐ Please send brochure.

Name (please print)

Company

Address

IBM *Electric Typewriters*
TRADE-MARK
INTERNATIONAL BUSINESS MACHINES CORPORATION

**1960s
Allied
Ironfounders
Advert**

I'm not sure
George is so
confident about his
gift – looks like he's
poised for a quick
exit through the
window in case she
throws it at him.

ISN'T
GEORGE
SWEET... Leaving it there for me to find. He knew how
I hated our old sink. And now this heavenly surprise. Leisure of all
things. Nothing but the best for George. It looks so right and is so
sensible. That ultra-deep bowl. Positively masses of draining board.
And such a wonderful white. Obviously designed by a woman. But
it was bought by my George. Bless him!   IN WHITE OR COLOURED VITREOUS
ENAMEL FROM £6.6.0 OR STAINLESS STEEL (FITTINGS EXTRA). MADE FOR LEISURE OR OTHER CABINETS.

Allied Ironfounders LEISURE
Leisure Works, Long Eaton, Notts.
NAME
ADDRESS
HWLS1/11
SHOWROOMS: 146 REGENT STREET, LONDON W1

LEISURE SINKS MADE BY **ALLIED IRONFOUNDERS**

Acknowledgements

All the images used in this book were provided by the Advertising Archives, except p37, which was kindly supplied by Minnie Fingerhut. Thanks to the companies and products featured for permission to reproduce their adverts. Particular credits are as follows:

p58 reproduced by kind permission of White Castle System, Inc., All Rights Reserved. p61 reproduced by kind permission of the National Confectioners Association.

Every effort has been made to trace the copyright holders of the images reproduced. Any further information pertaining to copyright will be included in future editions.

First published in 2007 by New Holland Publishers (UK) Ltd
London • Cape Town • Sydney • Auckland

10 9 8 7 6 5 4 3 2 1

www.newhollandpublishers.com

Garfield House, 86–88 Edgware Road, London W2 2EA, UK
80 McKenzie Street, Cape Town 8001, South Africa
Unit 1, 66 Gibbes Street, Chatswood, NSW 2067, Australia
218 Lake Road, Northcote, Auckland, New Zealand

ISBN: 978 1 84537 980 3

Publishing Director: Rosemary Wilkinson
Commissioning Editor: Seth Edwards
Project Editor: Kate Parker
Cover design: Ken Griffiths
Design: Zoë Mellors
Production: Melanie Dowland

Reproduction by Modern Age Repro House Ltd, Hong Kong
Printed and bound by Craft Print International Pte Ltd, Singapore